Modern Death: The End of Humanity

Carl-Henning Wijkmark

Modern Death: The End of Humanity

Carl-Henning Wijkmark

Translated by Dan Farrelly

Carysfort Press, Dublin

A Carysfort Press Book in association with Peter Lang

Modern Death: The End of Humanity
by Carl-Henning Wijkmark
Translated from the German Senftenberg Version 2006
by Dan Farrelly
First published in Ireland in 2007 as a paperback original by
Carysfort Press, 58 Woodfield, Scholarstown Road
Dublin 16, Ireland
ISBN 978-1-78874-887-2
©2006 Copyright remains with the author

Typeset by Carysfort Press
Cover design by Alan Bennis

This book is published with the financial assistance of
The Arts Council (An Chomhairle Ealaíon), Dublin, Ireland

Carysfort Press acknowledges the financial assistance of
Ireland Literature Exchange (Translation Fund), Dublin, Ireland
www.irelandliterature.com
info@ irelandliterature.com

Performing rights: all professional and amateur rights for this play are strictly reserved. Application for permission for performance should be made before rehearsals begin to: Carysfort Press.

Caution: All rights reserved. No part of this book may be printed or reproduced or utilized in any form or by any electronic, mechanical, or other means, now known or hereafter invented including photocopying and recording, or in any information storage or retrieval system without permission in writing from the publishers.

Translator's Note

Carl-Henning Wijkmark's original text, published in Swedish in 1978, was translated into German by Hildegard Bergfeld and published by the Gemini Verlag Berlin in 2001. In 2006 the Senftenberg Theatre Company adapted the piece for the German stage. The present English translation is based, by kind permission, on the Senftenberg version.

Dramatis personae:

A Moderator
Mr Bert Persson, Ministerial Director
Dr Storm, Institute for Medical Ethics (female)
Mr Axel Rönning, historian of Intellectual Sciences and writer
Dr Carnemo, theologian (female)
A recorder of minutes

Moderator: Ladies and Gentlemen! I would like to welcome you all to this symposium on the theme of 'The last phase of a human life'. The symposium was organized by DELLEM. DELLEM is the project group in the Social Ministry dealing with particular questions regarding the last phase of human life.

When we sent out our invitations and information we also named some ground rules to be observed in such conferences involving issues which public opinion treats as sensitive. I hope you will not take it amiss if I briefly remind you. Above all, this is a closed conference: the media have no access to it, and what is dealt with here may only be communicated to them – now and also later – with my approval. Second: everyone is requested not to leave the conference without a serious reason. Experience has shown that continued presence of [all members] is of great importance for maintaining contact in the discussion and thus for the outcome of the whole symposium. That was the unpleasant part. We hope that the enjoyment of one another's company will compensate for it.

The last phase of human life: this covers an extraordinarily broad spectrum of questions, from theology and philosophy to sociology, biology, and chemistry. And so I am especially happy to welcome our invited participants, who have agreed to expound for us their points of view. We are grateful to them for thus giving us a means of testing our ideas.

I welcome Ministerial Director, Mr Bert Persson; Dr Storm from the Institute for Medical Ethics; the historian of Intellectual Sciences, and writer, Mr Axel Rönning; and the theologian, Dr Carnemo.

In his introductory paper Mr Persson will give an overview of the problems and a political orientation which reflects the Social Ministry's point of view. Then we will have two lectures. Dr Storm will speak about social and nursing ethics, and Mr Rönning will give what he calls a review of the history of human dignity. But first, Mr Persson.

Ministerial Director Persson: Ladies and Gentlemen! In this early stage of our new plans we are happy to put out feelers in different directions to gather criticism and knowledge through informal discussion, for the questions about the last phase of human life are no longer the privileged domain of the doctors. Instead, shared economic concerns are to pave the way for necessary reforms. I don't need to describe the situation in much detail. A quick sketch should suffice. The population pyramid looks like a cigar, and if everything goes on as at present it will assume the form of a mushroom. The children we have been deprived of through abortions will reappear threefold at the top when we are old and unproductive. One person in four is on a pension by reason of age, and one person in eight has taken early retirement. 75% of care costs are for long-term care and for hopeless cases. Here the summit is reached and in the last ten to fifteen years has been passed. Amongst the 25%

of those who are productive and carry everything there are varying degrees of discontent, but this discontent has been gagged in two ways. The first is called the right to vote, and silences the politicians. Old people still have the right to vote, even if they live to be a hundred, and no party can afford to lose two million votes. The other is an old taboo and is called reverence for human life, and this silences everybody. And so all is quiet, although the pressure of taxes becomes increasingly unbearable, unemployment is on the increase, and a seemingly endless depression is consuming all but the bones of our society.

Perhaps one or other of you will feel uneasy.

Where is Persson heading? Don't worry. I haven't forgotten Hitler. We are not planning a mass murder of the old, the physically impaired, and other useless mouths to be fed. If Hitler achieved anything, it was that he made such thoughts impossible in Europe for the foreseeable future. The question is whether the very name of Hitler should, along with all that is associated with it, also block cautious and human selection, which is necessary to save a nation from decline. If that were the case he would have finally conquered us.

For decades we have been reckoning damage caused by alcohol, traffic accidents, and suicide, in terms of social costs for care and reduced production. Even those who are still angling for pensioners' votes by talking about more funds for long-term care, and about non-erosion of pensions and such-like things, finally fall back on an economic argument, namely, that the old have the right to a comfortable old age, because, it is said, they have built up this society. But what if their old age costs so much that they tear down again what they have built up? And now, when the economic situation is really bad, we have an explosion in the numbers of old people. Dying is seen as unnatural. More than ever. An important reason for this, of course, is that there has been great progress in the easing of pain. But we also have what is called the new fear of death, and we have to deal with this. We need a new attitude towards death and towards aging. It must again become natural to die when the active phase is over. We have to solve the problems *with* the old people, not *against* them.

One politician wanted to take away from pensioners their right to vote, along with their driver's license. But as long as they have the vote their numbers will be sufficient to out-vote such a suggestion. For the same reason it is not possible to lower their standard of living in any significant way. The politicians can get nowhere. As planners we have to help them to make a start.

So the situation is as follows: if we want security we have to be selective. And if we want to retain the system, compulsion is excluded. So what is left?

First I want, in a non-committal way, to sketch a feasible solution. My starting point is the following question – and again, I repeat, I have not forgotten Hitler – : How can society increase the readiness to die, the willingness of our target group to leave this life? For some that may perhaps sound utopian, as we in DELLEM thought before we started into it. But it is not utopian. It is only a question of avoiding a particular kind of political terminology. We took an opinion poll, naturally in a veiled form, involving a chosen group of pensioners. Especially in the groups which the politicians usually refer to as the weak members of society or as the little people, there is a latent readiness for reform in this area beyond all expectation. A community spirit that is admirable, if one considers the hard life experiences of these people. They are plagued by the thought of being in some way a burden to the community, not being able to provide long-term care for themselves and so on. Even by the age of seventy, when their energies decrease and the debilities that come with age set in, they begin to feel the pressure of the younger people; the burden of the crisis and of unemployment which is placed, so to speak, on the shoulders of the consuming group [the aged]. And the voice of the community, if we are careful to strengthen it, becomes so much stronger than that of their own will to live that they will, perhaps precisely as a final act of independence, ask to be allowed to end it.

Of course, this is only the beginning of a development which has to be steered with the help of patiently sifted information and enlightenment before a final solution can take shape. We at DELLEM want to apply to this final solution the well-known formula *voluntary obligation*. Naturally, by 'voluntary' I mean a centrally taken decision which is reached in a proper democratic process. What we want is a *social* solution: a right, established by law, to protection against prolonged old age and its hardship. Everyone should have the guarantee that, when they have reached a certain hopeless stage in sickness, helplessness, or weakness associated with age – or still better: earlier, when they have reached a fixed age limit – society should step in and administer a liberating and painless death. People should not have to beg for it. Before we are ready for a general age limit of seventy, or perhaps seventy-five, society can delegate individual decisions to composite parliamentary committees with a doctor as chairperson, following the model of our courts. Discussion about the modalities can continue, but in the meantime there is a long journey ahead of us, and, on the way, many stumbling blocks will doubtless have to be removed. But more have already been removed than most people think, very quietly. I can offer the example that for a long time now in our hospitals an unspoken instruction has been followed which allows for incomplete treatment of pensioners who have heart attacks. The same applies, quite officially, to the treatment of certain children who have severe impediments. This brings about savings we cannot ignore. In addition we have an area of privileged treatment in intensive care, about which Dr Storm will give us more detailed information.

Finally, I would like to point out a few stumbling blocks which doubtless still exist. As is well known, since the 1960s society has carried out intensive health campaigns on a broad scale. Health checks, calls for fitness, better working conditions, enlightenment of people about alcohol and tobacco, propaganda for certain kinds of nourishment and so on. All with the aim of increasing productivity and reducing the burden on the health-care system. But in a time of economic crisis like ours, with its increasing unemployment, all this leads to a painful contradiction. We have produced people who not only live longer but also retain their productive capacity much longer. And now we are sitting here with a crowd of well-trained pensioners who could very easily keep on working and would also do so if they were given the chance. But you can't have that. There are not enough jobs and there is pressure from the unemployed young people. But the old people live on even without working. They are physically fit and mobile, and they are storing up enough health and energy to last for decades. And for all this outdated and completely useless life-energy society is paying ever higher storage costs: 60 billion a year at present. And that has to be paid by taxing the active population. And if we now get to see a generation of hundred-year-olds it will finally be the task of long-term care to look after them, if only because no abstinence in the world can help them to remain clear-headed. And so we have, alongside the political problem, a vicious circle.

But for the moment I would like to leave it there.

Moderator: I would like to thank Mr Persson for his introductory thoughts which, as he told me beforehand, he intentionally delivered in an unsystematic way to avoid setting tracks which might impede a fresh and lively exchange of ideas. The discussion needs to have the openness and daring which the situation demands. We need a new impulse. And now: Doctor Storm of the Institute of Medical Ethics.

Dr Storm: Thank you. I will take up immediately what for me was the central point of Mr Persson's remarks: the question of economics and ethics, social values and human values. I will begin with three choice situations, three constructs, which I also use as examples in my teaching. Imagine an intensive care unit in the country which only has facilities to deal with one patient. In the first example, a serious case of brain haemorrhage is delivered in with a 10% chance of survival. While he is on the machine a traffic accident case comes in with a 50% chance of survival. The case is clear: the brain haemorrhage has to give way. We have made a choice based on the doctor's judgement of the chances of survival. There was no evaluation of human worth. In the next example there is the choice between two people with the same chances of survival. One of them is mentally deficient and the other is a Nobel prize winner. The choice in this case is equally obvious. Here, too, I have never encountered a doctor who, idealistically, would hesitate to save the Nobel prize winner. Here we have an evaluation both of human worth and of what I call social value. I will come back to the subject of the human worth of the mentally deficient. It would be interesting to hear what Mr Rönning has to say. And also Doctor Carnemo, who is a theologian.

My third example is more complicated. Three emergency cases are brought in on the same night. The first is a girl about twenty years old, a pianist with the promise of a brilliant career in the music world. The staff go to work with keenness and dedication. But then a new patient is announced: a forest worker about forty-five years old. A data check shows that the girl is single, while the forest worker has a wife and four dependent children. A judgement of human worth is not required here. The social value, or, if you prefer it, the value to the community, comes down in favour of the father of the family. Now, our man is lying on the operating table, and the staff are preparing for his operation. In comes, on this hectic night, a traffic accident with life-endangering injuries. He is a government politician. He is holidaying in the area, is drunk, and has driven into a tree. He is sixty years old and a bachelor. According to the Catholic moral view, which I agree with in this case, the right choice is to prefer him to the forest worker lying on the operating table.

Why? We don't have to go into the question of human worth, and from the point of view of value to the general community the politician clearly doesn't rate very well. But the social value of a leading politician can be considered so great that he is given the highest priority. He has to be saved for the sake of the State, which in modern reckoning is the highest of all values. He beats even the Nobel prize winner, whose discoveries, if he is a scientist, naturally can have great material value – but in general of a more diffuse, long-term, and international kind. If he is a Nobel prize winner for literature, in principle he sinks to the same level as our pianist, i.e., he has a cultural, aesthetic, and hobby-type social value.

Those are my three examples. As you see, they are constructed with a view to highlighting different scales of value. Now, of course, it would be possible to claim that not only a serious mental disturbance – the mentally deficient – but also chronic asociality and criminality, in the same way as advanced old age, indicate a low level of human worth. In relation to serious criminals, an overwhelming percentage of the population would support such a judgement. The same probably applies in relation to the aged, even if an objective statement of the people's opinion on the issue is hard to imagine, given the taboos which Mr Persson has touched on. If we were to pass on to the clearer and more neutral concept of social value perhaps greater openness would be possible.

The strategy I want to suggest has precisely this as its aim. This selection problem, if you want to call it that, becomes demystified when you move it from the ultimately metaphysical and therefore arbitrary scale of human values to the social scale which is, in practice, more manageable. Here, rational and quantitative measurements are really possible and can be reduced to learnable routines.

But perhaps I have moved on too quickly. There must still be those for whom all comparative evaluations of people must be condemned as unethical bartering. In the inevitable crisis situations when personnel and equipment are in short supply one would above all like to avoid making a rational choice and leave the decision to less rational powers, like chance or fate or God – if one has a metaphysical bent. But if one follows my suggestion, i.e. takes human worth out of the firing line and replaces it with social value in its different aspects – thus following a strategy of pragmatic ethics – one avoids this dilemma. For the whole idea of absolute human value stands or falls with the Christian point of view. It is based on the Christian teaching of natural law. But even the two main Christian confessions are prepared in certain cases to make exceptions regarding human value. In any case, people are not inflexible. I would like to elucidate this further, so as to cover myself in this matter.

In one of his table talks Luther said that he was once shown a twelve-year-old child who was mentally deficient. He had immediately suggested that the child be killed. It was a useless creature that did nothing but eat and ate as much as four farmers or farm workers. He thought that such changelings were only a piece of meat, a *massa carnis* with no soul in it. The devil had taken over the place of the soul, and so the child was a monster, not a human being, and could be killed without fear of punishment. The fifth commandment –

Dr Carnemo: That is, of course, typical of the time. People believed in small demons ...

Mr Rönning: Is it not rather typical of Luther? Luther was brutal. I know this story very well. Doctor Storm did not quote the part in which Luther said to the few Princes who happened to be present, 'If I were Prince or ruler here I would personally drown the child in the river'. And the Princes emphatically rejected this, disgusted by its brutality. If you compare this with Jesus in similar situations –

Dr Carnemo: You can't do that, and you have to realize that Luther was often given to exaggeration in his table talk. Quite simply, he was not always sober. The Lutheran Church is absolutely not committed to this utterance of his.

Mr Rönning: But it has played a terrible role in German history. One of the worst of German medical criminals used this passage to justify the murder of fifty-six children during the war. And some of them were *not* mentally deficient.

Moderator: Are we not getting off the point? Perhaps we should let Doctor Storm continue.

Mr Rönning: May I just ask Doctor Carnemo whether she disagrees with Luther's view when it is a case of the human value of mentally deficient or monstrous or mongoloid children?

Dr Carnemo: That's not what I said. I wanted to distance myself from his callous mode of expression. Luther was no gentle humanist. But where there is no life of a human soul we are not dealing with a human being. These children are a cruel game of nature, and their life has nothing in it but suffering for themselves and for others. Dr Storm's claim that we would be making exceptions to the dogma of human value if we let these children avail of help to die without pain is too narrow a view. Speaking of human values presupposes precisely the Christian teaching about natural law and creatures with human reason and a soul. Here we can draw parallels with brain-death. That does not stop us from showing mercy to all creatures.

Mr Rönning: Thank you. In my own presentation I will come back to these questions.

Moderator: Now, please, Dr Storm.

Dr Storm: I am really grateful for Dr Carnemo's enlightening comments about exceptions from human values. I am not sure whether Dr Carnemo has Catholicism behind her, but that is of no great importance.

Dr Carnemo: But it is!

Dr Storm: Anyway. I'd like to come back to my main idea. We have to face the terrible dilemma: either to give our own grandfather an extra month to survive or, for the same expense to give maybe ten children in a poor country the chance of living a whole life. Looked at from this point of view the thought processes sketched out by Mr Persson are in no way shocking. So, when our active time is over and when we have been allowed, as pensioners, to enjoy a suitable amount of time in peace and diversion, it should be time for us to express our thanks for what we have had and to die with dignity. One could even say: doing this would make our death dignified. But there is always the exception to be made for our political leaders and for other key persons in our society. The great task for the next ten years will be – and I am convinced of this – to introduce this new life and death ethic, which, properly understood, does not lessen our respect for human values but increases it: the human value of others.

Let us consider an example: chronic dialysis is for us, too, a selection problem of the highest order. We have dialysis machines for ten per cent of the patients who need them. The others die. Why are there so few machines? Naturally, they are expensive because they tie up care resources for a long period, in some cases for years until a transplant is possible. Above all, investing in these patients hardly pays off. They rarely become fully employable.

So, if the resources are not sufficient to save all patients, either it has to be left to chance to determine who has to die or a rational selection has to be made involving a comparative evaluation of human life. There is no third possibility.

Let us take the group of children whom we refer to in daily conversation as mongoloid, but whom I prefer – out of respect for the Mongols – to call children with Downs Syndrom, or – out of respect for the children – Downs Syndrom cases. For these mentally deficient, these imbeciles, are not children at all and will never be human in the sense of conscious persons. Even if they reach adult age, which is unusual. And what follows from that? That nothing ought to be done, and also nothing *is* done, to prolong the life of these creatures. You smooth the way to a passive euthanasia by leaving out normal inoculations and medical treatment. But should we not be able to go further? Should we not be given legal authority to give a merciful death precisely to these children as soon as they are born? And should this not be done also as a mercy to the parents? Would not suggesting such legislation be an excellent test of the preparedness of public opinion finally to accept limits to blind vitalism where human life is concerned?

Moderator: Thank you Dr Storm. It is immensely important where one draws the line. The physically impaired are very well organized and eloquent. What would happen if they were to storm the mass media and cause a set-back to the whole question of assisted death? Would that not lead to the creation of further taboos protecting all unproductive groups, including the aged? That would result in putting a stop to reforms which could not be countered until the whole economy is destroyed. Mr Persson, do you see here a possible weakness in the step-by-step tactics of Dr Storm?

Mr Persson: To prevent this escalation perhaps we have, above all, to drive in a wedge between the physically handicapped and the healthy or only between the physically feeble old people on the one hand – the psychologically handicapped, perhaps including drug addicts and habitual criminals – and senile old people on the other. Through proper education we could in the long run bring public opinion to the point where such categories are acceptable.

Dr Storm: So in this you are giving up your own idea of a general capping of old age limit along with the idea of a voluntary obligation.

Mr Persson: Yes, I've had some doubts. Let me start from the beginning. The selection will be made according to what you call social value. All right.

You are saying now, if I have understood you correctly, that the categories of the monstrous children and those unfit for life have been expanded to include marginal groups – first and foremost those of the mentally deficient. That would be a leap from 5,000 to 40,000. But how can their lives be taken without it being noticed? No, Dr Storm, this solution is not practicable. We have to follow the other course: bringing psychological influence to bear on the old so that they themselves want to put an end to things. Directly and through what we can call community spirit. A new way of thinking, a new social institution based on the will of the people.

Why should we not treat the last day of a person's life as a day of celebration? Think of the village communities of old. When the old people noticed that they had played their part and that their powers were at an end, they took leave of their relatives and of the inhabitants of the village. It was a small, moving village feast in which the old people, perhaps for the only time in their lives, were the focus of attention. They themselves led the procession to the cliff of death and ceremoniously handed over the tribe's club, which had been handed down through the generations, to the representatives of the village. Solidarity, shared responsibility was thereby very finely expressed, all having to hold the at least touch the club before the actual execution, which, according to the contemporary ways of thinking, was carried with the minimum possible pain. One for all and all for one. Youth, represented by the most beautiful girl – or boy, if it was a question of an old woman – played a special role and bade farewell to the old people with a kiss, called the kiss of death.

Dr Storm: No, Mr Persson, I think we can and should appeal to realism and healthy common sense and not try to control people's attitudes through suggestive propaganda.

Moderator: Go out into the houses with logical positivism, you are saying?

Dr Storm: Well, why not? Democracy would find it more palatable and it would be more in line with social development. My recipe is patient explanation rather than suggestion.

It should not be impossible to bring older people to the realization that they have had their fair share of life and have made their contribution to life. To say it once more: death must become natural again. The death of an old or hopelessly sick or handicapped person should not be seen as something bad that is to be avoided at all costs. How many of us who, as doctors or relatives, have witnessed at close quarters long-term care and the care of hopeless cases, and have not felt a deep desire to have them spared the human – or inhuman – suffering we see! To lie there like a wreck, an unappetizing packet, attached to various apparatuses, probes, infusions, respirators etc. When one was, perhaps, thriving creature with beautiful healthy limbs. In this context the expression 'quality of life' is a mockery, and it is nasty and shabby not to release these people from a so-called life that is nothing but humiliation and torture. So, not only as a member of society but also personally I have a sense of great relief to know that the question of long-term care is at last heading towards a solution.

Moderator: I believe Dr Storm and her institute for medical ethics are without doubt are important monitors in this area. It is reassuring that no hindrances are to be feared from this direction.

I would now ask the historian of ideas and writer, Mr Axel Rönning, to speak.

Mr Rönning: You will have realized that I belong, so to speak, to the enemy camp. The project group DELLEM has good reason to think that the tradition of ideas which I represent is as good as defunct. This being so, what is expected of me is a little bit of entertainment from the sphere of cultural history.

Moderator: Dear Mr Rönning, you are labouring under an illusion! We, let me say, hope that we can sharpen our arguments on the barriers you put in our way. We will give what you have to say our fullest attention.

Mr Rönning: All right. Let's look at death for a moment. Could we have the projector, please? Thank you.

Look at this skeleton with the wine jars in either hand. It is a floor mosaic of a dining room in Pompeii. That's what death looked like when it was really natural. A nice death that challenged us to enjoy life and to die with glass in hand. In our society this image could only be used as an anti-alcohol advertisement, for our modern death today has nothing in its hands; it has no hands, no shape. It is a hospital wall, empty and smooth and hygienic.

This friendly skeleton talks to us not just about the healthy hedonism of antiquity. It also speaks of the brevity of life. In antiquity people died young. They seldom lived more than forty years. For the very reason that life was so short people wanted to enjoy it as long as it lasted. There were no guarantees in life and there was no life after death. Without a care they built their cities beside Vesuvius. But we do that too. Or rather, we build Vesuvius near our cities – in the form of nuclear power plants.

We, too, have no hope of an after life since Christianity has been extinguished. Therefore we should seen on a level with the Pompeians, rejoice in life and look death straight in the eye. But we are not able to do that, and such a frivolous idea would not occur to Dr Storm or Mr

Persson. Enjoy life? That is not the way society sees it. Why not? Why are we not permitted what was permissible for the Pompeians?

But how do we know that the Pompeians were happier than we are? We cannot know it for sure, but there is an enormous collection of material evidence. Traces of life more beautiful than ours, objects which speak of joy and the life of the senses in rich variety.

Where *we* have shopping warehouses, boxes to sleep in and televisions, scattered around in the mud, the Pompeians had this wonderful variety: a society penetrated through and through by a suffiently strong culture. The quality of life was higher. No honest person can be in doubt about it. Hygiene and care of the sick was worse, of course, which accounts for the lower average life.

From this, selection followed in a so-called natural way, the selection that Dr Storm and Mr Persson would so happily put in the hands of society and that all the DELLEM committees in the whole world are so desperately trying to justify.

What is it, then, that we dislike about Pompeii? There was no mania for progress, no productionism. For that reason they had no need to be curbed by massive bureaucracies to prevent them landing in the abyss. They still had nature and no methods for plundering it. Now, when nature is approaching its end a small society is becoming attractive again. We want to produce less, says one side at the beginning of the 1970s. Let us become poorer and not put such a high price on the human person. Instead, let us have higher human values and a better quality of life. The aim was to have a cleaner environment, and one imagined that this had something to do with abstinence, with vegetarian insipidness. We would never have achieved a new Pompeii: the free, creative life with girls, drink, and refined culture; a life that was shorter but more human.

And then around 1980 these 'green' movements disappeared. They had come too late. Or perhaps not? Was it just that the states, the bureaucracies, and the interest of capital were too strong? We will never know. Atomic energy carried all before it. That was the crux of the matter. Today we find ourselves in a situation in which a project that sets in motion the two levers of this society – resources and justice – has every prospect of succeeding. Even if it is as frightfully barbaric as Mr Persson and Dr Storm have painted it. It releases enormous economic resources but guarantees at the same time a kind of macabre justice. The idea of an obligatory death in a certain sense realizes in its own way a democracy of death, which is certainly one of the oldest dreams of humanity. I find it hard to see what forces can stop this suggestion or even delay in any way worth mentioning. And so I think that Dr Storm's caution regarding the time-frame is unnecessary.

But I would have expected a bit of symbolic resistance from Dr Carnemo. –

We can have the lights now. Thank you.

What the ageing person feels about his death is really of no interest to them. They want him to accept as natural that he is superfluous to society, that if he remains any longer on earth he is useless, expensive, and harmful to society. I would like to call death as DELLEM understands it 'modern death', now that 'new death' seems to be a group name given by American professors who are waiting for a DNA genetic resurrection in refrigeration boxes.

Moderator: Just a moment! You have attacked the social state!

Mr Rönning: I am opposed to its being developed to its logically absurd conclusions.

Security has become a fetish, a trap for freedom. A twenty-year-old who, in choosing a career, is already speculating about his pension advantages, has already given up on life. Security is our imprisonment in the bureaucracy which feeds off it. Security is the tragedy of the workers' movement and of society in general. This is one of the main causes of stagnation lack of vitality. It seems now to be leading to the 'rock of death'.

Mr Persson: It could be that with certain reforms we have gone too far. But they are not meant as attacks on bureaucracy but on democracy. And in our system reforms cannot be revoked, so there is no point in criticizing them afterwards. It is a question of finding new solutions, and that is what we are attempting. Your criticism is too superficial. It is easy to be an anarchist.

May I slot in here something about the 'new death'? Isn't it true that people who now live in the Western world have gained some idea of physical immortality or, at any rate, of a radical prolongation of life through the new genetic research? In this case a massive selection takes place in which the physically, but above all the intellectually better placed people are chosen for survival.

Is it mere chance that in recent years there has been an enormous flood of Who's Who publications? Is this whole business not an appeal to the vague hopes of belonging to the chosen ones while the others are left to die the natural way?

Mr Rönning: That is certainly a good observation. But what do you conclude from it?

Mr Persson: If we take our standard selection, according to which all agree not to live beyond the age of 70 or perhaps 75, we will perhaps be spared this luxury selection with its terrible injustices.

Mr Rönning: Both kinds of selection are repugnant. And this one, which you call luxury selection, is undoubtedly more unjust. But at least it does not make murderers of us. And perhaps in fifty years time, as many involved in research of the future believe, there will be a third selection: hunger selection.

Moderator: But the other two kinds of selection want to forestall that one. Mr Persson.

Mr Persson: And so we should prefer the method of selection we aiming at. Don't you see the corollary to the genetic solution? A horde of Supermen ruling over millions of slaves. That was the world state that Hitler dreamed of, and we are distancing ourselves from it.

Mr Rönning: I am glad of that. But the lesser evil you are choosing is, in spite of everything, is based on murder which will become usual practice. We start to slaughter one another to escape a catastrophic famine which will perhaps turn us into cannibals. What wonderful prospects for the future!

Moderator: But let me come back to the modern death, the one for our time, the one that today DELLEM nurturing.

Mr Rönning: O.K. Since the Second World War 'modern death' has seriously gained ground in the West and it still operates mainly with technology and regulatory methods developed at that time. Computer technology is the only really significant addition. It has geared itself to making people's lives as dead as possible, above all by the production of unnecessary and meaningless goods. It kills our imagination and joy for living, organizes us from above, prevents us from organizing ourselves, creates activities to prevent us from being active. It fills our spare time with a puritanical materialism in which the life of the senses and every chance of experiencing pleasure are eradicated. It forces us to live in a death-like world of motorways and concrete tunnels, in houses made of concrete and travel resorts made of plastic. Life death in advance. It is death on borrowed money which you pay back in instalments.

But now the impulses of the Second World War are ebbing away. There is a noticeable lack of ideas. Large-scale wars no longer offer practicable solutions. Small wars are not to be despised, but they are difficult to keep under control.

Moderator: DELLEM and its many related committees world-wide are to be seen in this context. Modern death has set its monitoring bodies and specialists the task of liquidating, in a peaceful form, the old and other superfluous consuming individuals. Collective and unified solutions are, as always, to be recommended.

Mr Rönning: Let me play the visionary for a moment and arrive at the day on which I myself cross the age-line and it is my turn to be brought into the death clinic. My doorbell rings, I open, and see the agents, the pimps of death. Perhaps the interior of the ambulance is comfortable, perhaps there is a small state ceremony on arrival. But it makes no difference what verbiage is used in the ritual. I will understand the real message, which is: 'We've got you now, you dog! We were not able to kill off your life altogether, but now, at your death, we are going to do things properly. Individual? Integrity? Now you will be sucked in, now you are here, now you will pay for putting conscience before conformity, imagination before routine, freedom before security, the world before isolation; in short, for not being dead enough. Now you are one of us, just as dead as we are. Now you are to become dung and finally of some little use. Take him away and bring the next one. Here activity is promoted, here room is made for security. Youth has pride of place.

Moderator: That was a kind of parenthesis, a personal expression of what Mr Rönning feels about the development of society as it has been presented here this morning. Mr Persson and Dr Storm and the others from DELLEM will, of course, distance themselves subjectively from such a view.

Mr Rönning: But that is the way I see, and I think many feel the same. Those who either because of weakness or stubbornness today find themselves on the margins of our society. But I think that DELLEM, for this very reason, has little to fear from such opinions.

Mr Persson: But, dear Mr Rönning, we respect all your humanistic engagement. Why so much bitterness and pathos?

Mr Rönning: In the Sermon on the Mount, at the very heart of his Gospel, the poor in spirit are in the very front ranks of those deemed blessed. 'For theirs is the Kingdom of Heaven.' It is clear that precisely because of these words the poorest of the poor in spirit, the mentally deficient children escaped mass murder until Hitler's time.

It is correct that human values stand or fall with natural law. Modern history gives us terrible proof of this. On the other hand it is false that Christianity has a monopoly on the natural law idea, as Dr Storm believes. Natural law predates and postdates Christianity.

Moderator: We were all born at the same age, so why shouldn't we all die at the same age?

Dr Storm: Excuse me! May I add something before we leave the mentally deficient children? It is very rewarding and easy to be so fixed in one's principles as Mr Rönning is. But who is to look after these children and at what cost? Think of the suffering of the parents and siblings who have such a child in the home. And if they are cared for in an institution the cost for the community at large is enormous. Think of all the children in the developing world who could be kept healthy and fed for this money. We can no longer carry these meaningless burdens. We must favour those who are fit for life.

Mr Rönning: And all I can say in reply is that we must somehow carry these burdens if we want to retain our humanity. We will have to put a higher tax on wanton car-driving and, for all I care, on spirits and tobacco. Surely it is worth that much to retain human values and to avoid co-responsibility in legalized murder.

Nothing can be more a thing of the past in our society than the declaration of human rights made by the French National Assembly in 1789, so to be sure of accuracy I will quote the famous first paragraph: 'All people are born and remain free and equal in all rights.' Are born and remain: so the step is made from birth with human value and human rights, which they are to have for their whole lives even if they live to become 150 years old. [It applies to] from the fundamental equality in Christianity right up to the social market economy. With this step natural law has passed from the rulers to the ruled.

I hardly need to add, that this 'are born and remain' is a condemnation of the whole philosophy of DELLEM and all its plans to talk us into the death of the aged and the killing of the people referred to as worthless and unfit for life.

'Right is what is useful for the German people', Hitler used to say. That is exactly the same idea as when Dr Storm says that human value, as she calls it, has to yield to social value.

Mr Persson: Dr Storm can speak for herself, but I must protest against these constant comparisons with the totalitarian regimes of the past. Should it be possible – just by mentioning Hitler or Stalin – to block solutions which are required in a totally different situation? How long do we have to keep on denying that Hitler had many good ideas? And then this talk of murder in connection with the age politics we are planning and discussing here. Why are we not able to discuss age control or, if you like, death control just as much as we discuss birth control? Mr Rönning's historical exposé is interesting, but where do we end up if, in a completely changed world, we let ourselves be bound by history's constraints?

Moderator: DELLEM came into being to look for other solutions, and if we achieve it we will do it through explanation and persuasion. What we are aiming at is agreement on the part of the aged to end their lives earlier. And we believe that that happens best under the aegis of social solidarity, in a simple appeal to the 'We' feeling.

Mr Rönning: Yes, of course. Mr Persson portrayed the death rock like this, almost like a nice folk celebration. That is Dr Storm's 'society-oriented ethics of utilitaristic consistency: 'The common good takes precedence over the individual good.' Right is what is useful to society as a whole. So we are back with Hitler, whether Mr Persson likes it or not. A totally different situation, says Mr Persson. On the contrary, it was very similar to the present situation: depression, unemployment. And Hitler attacked it with methods which were quite similar to those of Mr Persson. Admittedly he did not go at the aged. Perhaps he would have managed that, too, if he could have lived – and operated – longer. Instead, he found other innocent groups. The Jews, the mentally deficient, later the Russian prisoners of war, who were murdered in their millions.

Let us take an imaginary scenario: that we have received scientific proof that different peoples have different value – the criterion of value being the capacity for practical intellectual achievement. Would we not have to forget about these proofs and go on living as usual and treat the fiction of the equal value of the races as a reality because otherwise the world would be unbearable? I would like to hear your answer to this.

Dr Storm: It is difficult to answer such hypothetical questions. But if we gave free rein to such fictions the final result would be total hypocrisy. Think of Brecht's Galileo play. The Church knew that he was right but it forced him to recant so as not to make people unhappy by shattering their faith in religion. Similarly with Kant, who presupposed there was a God because otherwise there would be no motivation for acting justly here on earth. That is a solution which impossible in our society, since it requires an authoritarian society of the bad old kind.

Mr Rönning: You are right about Galileo, because in that case people were to be kept in ignorance about a fiction. Only the elite were allowed to know the truth. But Kant was a man of the Enlightenment. Fictions that were required for the preservation of humanity should have been conscious. That would have been the task of the public culture. But we no longer have any public culture.

The Nürnberg trials were in the beginning an admirable attempt to place these principles at the centre of political morality. As an institution the Court was a twin of the United Nations, but after a few years it was dissolved. This was opportunism: Germany was to be re-armed. Another reason was that the Allies were not able to meet the norms which they themselves had established. The Vietnam War shows that.

Dr Storm: A question. Are we going to allow peace and coexistence to be threatened in the name of abstract justice?

MrRönning: 'If justice declines there is no point in men living on earth', says Kant. He also says, by the way, that it is better that one man die for the people than that the whole people be ruined.

Dr Storm: So now natural law has become negotiable?

Mr Rönning: It is tragic that medical ethics lends itself to the process of attacking a series of the most important human barriers – the barrier against selection.

Dr Storm: I am glad that Mr Rönning, in spite of everything, sees that we have to change the criteria from case to case.

Mr Rönning: Retirement is the only time in life in which one can decide for oneself and have a chance to live. That's why I am hoping for a protest from the old people, a resistance movement against the expectations of society that they shut their mouths, save their money, and die at the right time. On the day we retire let us move away from isolation and squander every cent in a more human country. Love, discover, eat, and drink, and elude the obligatory death.

Moderator: Many thanks, Mr Rönning, for the many interesting views. You must not think that we don't value your collaboration here. We are listening to your exaggerations calmly. But you are almost entirely wrong in your estimation of us. Dr Storm is trained in the humanities, and even I like to read poetry, look for mushrooms, listen to Vivaldi, if I have time. It is just that we average citizens cannot afford to live from culture alone, as you and a small handful of others are privileged to do. We have to find concrete solutions to concrete, burning questions. But Mr Rönning uncovered a possible breeding ground of opinions which are not to be underestimated or simply brushed aside just because of their mainly emotional character – which, on the contrary, makes them all the more dangerous because they can give rise to a kind of (let me say it) limited psychosis.

I'm sorry that I must interrupt the discussion when it is so gripping, but it is time for a coffee break. Let's say twenty minutes ...

BREAK

But today we also want to present a project that at DELLEM we call the B-Project. The B-Project is, so to speak, a part project. Not an alternative to the broader plan we outlined earlier, but rather a step on the way but at the same time with a goal in itself with its own economic implications. Mr Persson, please.

Mr Persson: I want to say from the beginning that this project can not be as open to debate as was unquestionably the case with regard to the main project. Human value is not at issue. I can give reliable assurance of that – for Mr Rönning's peace of mind. The doubts which, despite everything, can still be there are those of an entirely different level: the level of prescriptive law.

Let me begin with the medical and industrial part. In caring for the sick we have long been making transfers from person to person: of blood, tissue, and, in the case of transplants, whole organs. Here we find ourselves to a certain extent in a borderland between life and death. We cross the border altogether when it comes to using organs taken from, so to speak, totally dead persons for pharmaceutical purposes, or when we use whole bodies for purposes of research and teaching. In other words, a kind of salvaging. Why, we have asked ourselves, should we not be able to systematize this salvaging? To go one step further from organs to whole bodies, not just for the good of anatomical institutions but for the wider benefit of research and for utilization in industry. The question now is: how do we gain access to the bodies? We know that the majority of relatives are not willing to release the bodies of the departed for anatomical purposes. Anyone who has thought about it at all perhaps assumes that the corpse of a dead person belongs to the heirs. But that is not the case. Of course, relatives have rights over the body, but only with regard to burying it some way or other, in accordance with the directives in force. But even the state has no rights of possession, no rights regarding the disposal of the body. The body of a dead person has, quite simply, no rightful owner.

Moderator: But first, what religious views are there about this matter? I would like to ask Dr Carnemo briefly to give us some guidance here.

Dr Carnemo: Any resistance it is naturally on the traditional and emotional level. But since the Christian denominations have allowed cremation these feelings and traditions no longer have any real foundation. For reason and moral theory it can make no difference whether it is through fire or industrial salvage that the body ceases to exist. From a moral point of view the latter is preferable, because in this way the dead person renders a final service to his fellow men.

From the point of view of dogma there are no problems. We Lutherans and Evangelical Christians have never believed in the resurrection of the body.

Perhaps it is an expression of our traditional animosity towards the flesh. Catholics, on the other hand, have always liked to think that the dead, when the trumpets at the Last Judgement sound, quickly gather together their bones and rise up out of their graves as a skeleton, as we see it in medieval images. But not even they could make a dogma out of it. Still, out of sheer respect for tradition the Vatican fought hard against cremation and only permitted it in times of epidemic and of major catastrophe. But finally, in 1964, the Pope lifted the ban on cremation. Now it is probably only an old Jewish sect that adheres to it.

Even less can I see any hindrance to plans to use material and substances which will be of benefit to the living. On the contrary, I see a positive Christian kernel in this idea: a helping hand beyond the grave as an expression of love which is not earthly. God loves a cheerful giver. I think we should enter into this with an open mind.

Moderator: Many thanks, Dr Carnemo. May I ask you, Mr Persson, to come back to the economic aspect?

Mr Persson: Our specialists have discovered a direct salvage possibility which is ingenious in its simplicity. We had contact with researchers in the pharmaceutical industry who gave us information about important materials which up to now could be obtained from parts of animals. For example, heparin against blood-clotting, insulin and adrenalin against asthma etc, thyroxin against certain metabolic illnesses, and in addition: liver medicines against pernicious anaemia. And several other important substances which, in certain cases, are life-saving. If human bodies are available it would be possible to produce all of this – and much else – in better quality, much more cheaply, and probably in much larger quantities. Since taken from human beings, these substances would, so to speak, from the very beginning be programmed for the human organism.

Think of all the sleeping pills and tranquillizers we give people, especially in the last phase of their lives and in long-term care. They are stored up in the brain and only need to be mined. Gold.

And speaking of gold, reference has been made several times to the resources which are lost if we are not concerned about the gold teeth of the dead. These are undoubtedly resources. A kind of gold reserve.

If I move on to soil enrichment and the nourishment aspect: bone meal, bone glue, bone charcoal. For the chemical-technical industry in the broader sense fat is naturally attractive, but so is part of other materials. We don't know exactly which ones because it was difficult for us to arrange conversations with representatives of this branch. Great possibilities for the future, said the head of one research department. But he stressed very clearly that society must take the lead. If the State introduces it, it will be accepted, but if the initiative comes from the private sector there is always fierce resistance. Think of what happened to our colleagues in IG-Farben, he said.

So there we were again! The ghost of the past that Mr Rönning has so stubbornly conjured up. All right, if the Nazis killed the Jews to make soap out of them that naturally fills us with horror. On the other hand, to make soap, or whatever it is now, out of the fat of people who have died a natural death is quite another thing. In this case it is a question of producing and surviving a crisis.

Moderator: Dr Carnemo, can you wait a minute? We'll hear from you again very soon.

Mr Persson: What is the best way to proceed? From many discussions the concept 'terminal station' has evolved. A network of terminal stations is being set up and connected to health-care stations. We believe it is important to avoid the character of mass industry, which could lead to unpleasant associations. We want to have this activity as close to people as possible; we want to show that death can be productive, can give employment, and save threatened localities. This is the best way for us to deal with the unease and superstition which are still present.

The head of the terminal station will be a terminal director who ought to be an experienced administrator from the health-care sector. Alongside him there should be a head of research, preferably with the status of a professor, and a chief engineer as technical director responsible for the preparation sector. In addition, there should be scientific, technical, and administrative personnel, amounting to perhaps fifty people in each terminal station. For the various activities we can fall back on, amongst others, unemployed workers from the food industry, and for untrained young people the manual tasks could be an excellent preparation for a proper career in health-care, for, despite everything, it is people we are dealing with.

For the industrial utilization of raw materials and half manufactured products we have considered concessions for state and private enterprises, which would be best established in the same place. All refining should take place within the country.

There can be no doubt that the project is economically sound and that it will promote employment. And since crematoria will become virtually extinct, the project will save energy and be environment-friendly. After processing at the terminal stations, the insignificant remains of the human bodies which cannot be recycled or used as compost will be burned.

This has been a short sketch of the genuine advantages of the B-Project and its purely positive qualities. From the negative angle, if you so wish, solidarity and justice demand that no one refuses to meet this final social obligation of making his body available. It should not come to the point where privileged people, when they feel their end has come, take refuge abroad where the graves they have already bought await them.

Dr Storm: So escape of bodies abroad has to be prevented, and that requires restrictive measures. Above all, passports will have to be taken from the sick and feeble. A number of jobs for customs doctors will have to be created. Their task will be to examine at the border crossings suspects who are travelling abroad and, if appropriate, to stop them. Customs, disadvantaged for a long time now, is naturally looking forward to these new jobs with satisfaction.

Mr Persson: An important point for the formation of public opinion with regard to the B-Project is undoubtedly Nourishment-Movement-Health, above all from the point of view of hygiene. The ambition to leave behind perfectly satisfactory raw material could be the spur to living a healthier life style. You avoid introducing poisons into your body and your movements are no longer gratuitous, so to speak. Health campaigns have an obvious role to play in the salvaging programme when, but only when, a limit is set for age of death as discussed earlier. Otherwise society risks that the salvage gains will be swallowed up by the extra costs which come in the wake of an extended average age for living.

Let me now finally place the B-Project in a broader perspective. Is this not, in its way, the fulfilment of age-old dream: the ultimate social integration of death? On the other side there await no longer unknown powers but a continued, useful effort for the community in which we have lived. Instead of the eerie hush of the mortuary a workplace for production and research – is that not the proper meaning of the expression 'modern death'? Pulverized and thinly spread over the mighty field of society we will give it nourishment. Or what do you say, Mr Rönning?

Mr Rönning: It is true that dead people are not people any more. But by the same token neither are the raw material and products, not substances which can be made use of in this barbaric way. But I understand that for a mindset like that of Mr Persson an old dream becomes fulfilled when bodies which can no longer be exploited as means of production instead become products themselves. The saying goes that the priest's cows become fatter because they are allowed to graze in the cemetery.

Moderator: I did not really want to begin a discussion of the B-Project here and now. I wanted to ask you to think about it for a few weeks, each of you separately, and then send in your views in writing. And so ... Dr Carnemo? You wanted to say something?

Dr Carnemo: Something important has been forgotten here in the B-Project, namely that you have to have something to bury. Even if it is only a finger nail from the little finger, as sometimes happens after flooding catastrophes. The body may have the various stages of recovery to go through, but the journey of the soul is ended, and that is something we should mark by a dignified act of burial, as has happened in all generations before us.

From the Church's point of view it is an absolutely central question that the dead person be blessed and be laid to his final rest. The central council of the Church will never give up this demand. I cannot function as an expert for DELLEM if there is not a burial in some form or other.

Moderator: Let us hear your suggestion. That is a good way of closing the symposium.

Dr Carnemo: I have called it 'the little key to the Kingdom of Heaven', clavicula coeli. 'Clavicula', little key, is the Latin name for the collar bone.

It was customary to retain the collar bone of the dead person. It was given a special value. It is best if the celebrant wears a specially designed chasuble into which the key of Peter is woven. He holds the collar bone with both thumbs and forefingers high above his head and speaks the words, 'May this, XY, be a symbol for the key that will open to you the gate to the Kingdom of Heaven. Amen.' Then he lowers his hands to the metal urn and drops the collar bone into it with a ringing sound. This is taken up and magnified by the organ and answered with a chord, which, so to speak, becomes the dead person's own chord within the music of the spheres, the heavenly harmony. That's what I have in mind.

Moderator: That is certainly a lovely idea. I can guarantee you that we will come back to it.

Now. Many thanks to all of you. Go back home and think everything over. You will be hearing from us.

www.ingramcontent.com/pod-product-compliance
Ingram Content Group UK Ltd.
Pitfield, Milton Keynes, MK11 3LW, UK
UKHW022031210426
12012UKWH00003B/455